Disney
PRINCESS
1001
STICKERS

Autumn
Publishing

Cinderella Dress-up

Place the gloves and necklace stickers from your sticker sheet onto Cinderella so she can finally be ready for the ball.

True Shoes

Help Cinderella sort her glass slipper collection!
Only two of these pictures exactly match the
slipper in the centre. Find and circle them.

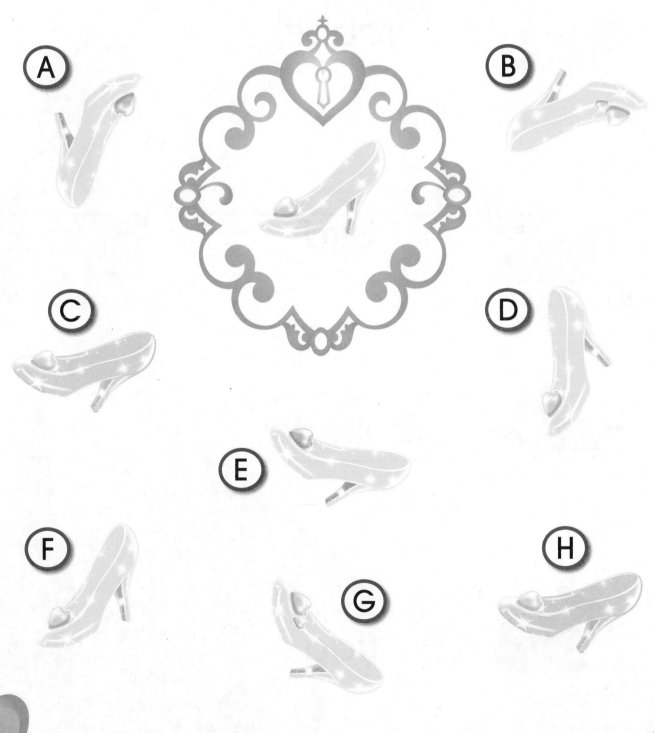

Answers on page 47

Cute Creatures

Princess Aurora loves creatures of all kinds!
Draw a line from each creature to its name.

A

B

C

D

1 **rabbit**

2 **bird**

3 **butterfly**

4 **frog**

Spot the Difference

There are five differences in the second picture of Aurora. Can you spot and circle them all?

Answers on page 47

Best Friends

Princess Jasmine's best friend is her pet tiger, Rajah. Can you spot eight differences between these two pictures?

Answers on page 47

Magic Carpet Fun

Aladdin has taken Jasmine on a magic-carpet ride! Decorate this beautiful scene using your pens and pencils.

Painting Patterns

Rapunzel has painted these pretty patterns. Can you work out which picture she should paint next in each row? Draw your answers in the boxes below.

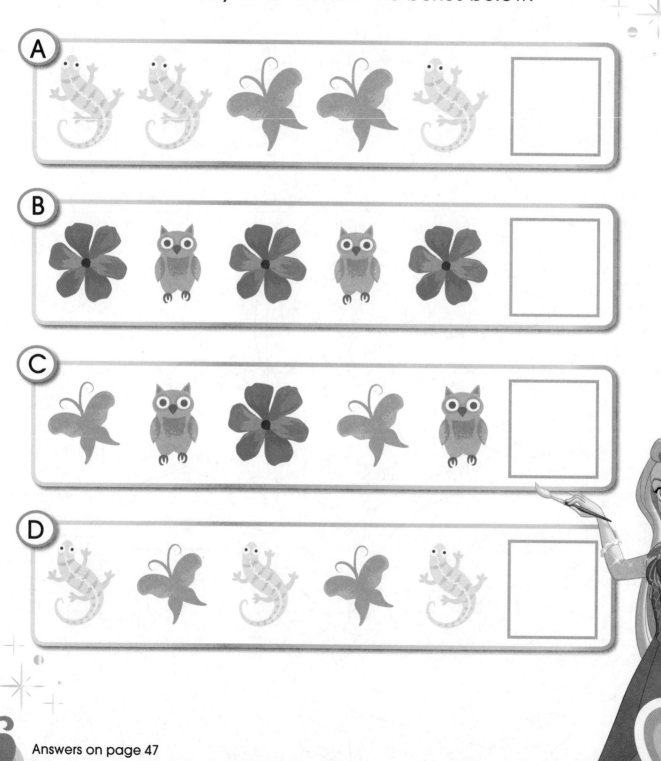

Where's Pascal?

Rapunzel's faithful friend, Pascal, has run off! Help Rapunzel find him by drawing the correct path through the maze.

START

FINISH

Answer on page 47

Time to Dance

Tiana and Prince Naveen love to dance! Only two of these pictures are exactly the same – can you spot the matching pair?

Answer on page 47

Terrace Jigsaw Fun

The happy pair are dancing on the terrace at Tiana's restaurant. Can you match the missing pieces to spaces in the picture?

Answer on page 47

Which Path?

Mulan wants to find her pet dog, Little Brother.
Which path should Mulan take to reach him?

Three-in-a-Row

Play this fun game with a friend! One of you is noughts (0) and the other is crosses (x). Take it in turns to fill a space in the grid. The winner is the first player to get three-in-a-row, either up, down, across or diagonally.

Dwarfs Mix-up

Help Snow White and the Seven Dwarfs put the images below in order so they match this happy scene.

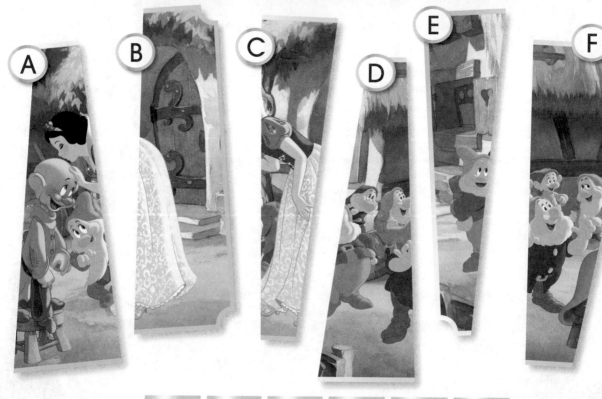

Princess Dressing

Help Snow White get ready for a day with the Seven Dwarfs.
Use your stickers to add her shoes, headband and top.

Colours of Nature

Pocahontas believes that every rock, tree and creature has a life of its own. Decorate this picture using your pens and pencils.

Beautiful Butterflies

Pocahontas and her friend, Meeko, love butterflies.
How many butterflies can you count on this page?

There are _____ butterflies.

Answer on page 47

Belle of the Ball

Use your mosaic stickers in the space below to design your very own ballroom floor for the Beast and Belle to dance on.

Special Day

Colour this picture of Belle and the Beast at the royal ball.

Brave Explorer

Merida loves to explore the Highlands on her horse, Angus.
Colour in this picture using your best pens and pencils.

True or False?

Use the boxes below to mark whether these sentences about Princess Merida are true or false.

	TRUE	FALSE
1. Merida lives in the Scottish Highlands.		
2. She has two little brothers, who are twins.		
3. Merida's horse is called Andrew.		
4. Merida is a very skilled archer.		
5. Merida believes in following your dreams.		

Answers on page 47

Under the Sea

Colour in this picture of Ariel swimming with her friends.

Underwater World

Ariel's home is a magical place. Spot and circle five differences in the picture on the right. Colour in a shell for every difference you find.

Answers on page 48

Creative Quiz

Unlock the artist inside! Starting at the top, answer 'yes' or 'no' to each question and follow the answers to discover what kind of creativity is right for you.

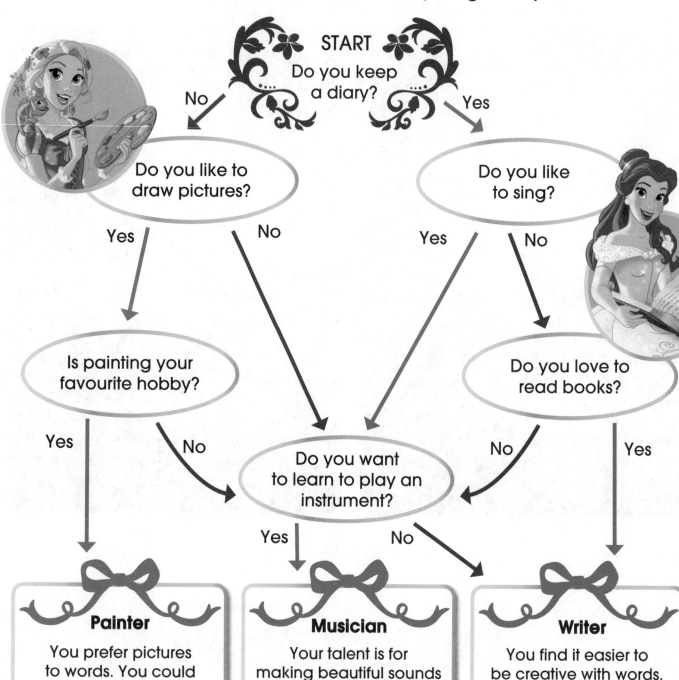

START
Do you keep a diary?

No → Do you like to draw pictures?

Yes → Do you like to sing?

Do you like to draw pictures?
- Yes → Is painting your favourite hobby?
- No → Do you want to learn to play an instrument?

Do you like to sing?
- Yes → Do you want to learn to play an instrument?
- No → Do you love to read books?

Is painting your favourite hobby?
- Yes → Painter
- No → Do you want to learn to play an instrument?

Do you love to read books?
- No → Do you want to learn to play an instrument?
- Yes → Writer

Do you want to learn to play an instrument?
- Yes → Musician
- No → Writer

Painter
You prefer pictures to words. You could be a famous artist!

Musician
Your talent is for making beautiful sounds with instruments.

Writer
You find it easier to be creative with words. You could write a novel.

Rapunzel's Heroes

Flynn and Maximus helped Rapunzel when she escaped from the tower. Match each of the close-ups to where they belong in the picture.

Answers on page 48

Dream Big

Tiana believes that wishes can open the doors to your dreams. Colour in this picture of the determined princess.

Tiana's Kitchen

Tiana is cooking some delicious food. Can you spot these items in her restaurant kitchen? Circle each of them.

- Green pear
- Red pepper
- Cherry pie
- Flowerpot

Answers on page 48

Complete the Scene

Mulan loves to sit by the water and dream.
Use your stickers to finish this peaceful scene.

Be Colourful!

Colour in this picture of Mulan as she chooses which beautiful fan to carry.

A Picture of Love

Snow White is happy to have met her true love. Look at this scene carefully, then answer the questions below.

1. How many Dwarfs are in the picture? _____

2. How many birds are in the picture? _____

3. What colour is Snow White's hair bow? _____

Answers on page 48

Who Am I?

What is this Dwarf's name? Write down the first letter then every third letter in the circle in the space below.

START HERE

H R S A B M O L P E S Y P T

__ __ __ __ __ __ __

Answer on page 48

Forest Friends

Pocahontas has two faithful animal friends – Meeko the raccoon and Flit the hummingbird. Can you match the missing heart pieces to the gaps in this picture?

1

2

3

4

A

B

C

D

Answer on page 48

Draw and Colour

Pocahontas loves talking to the animals in the forest.
Draw one of her animal friends, then colour in the picture.

Close-up Royalty

Can you tell which close-ups belong to Jasmine?
One of the close-ups doesn't belong. Which one is it?

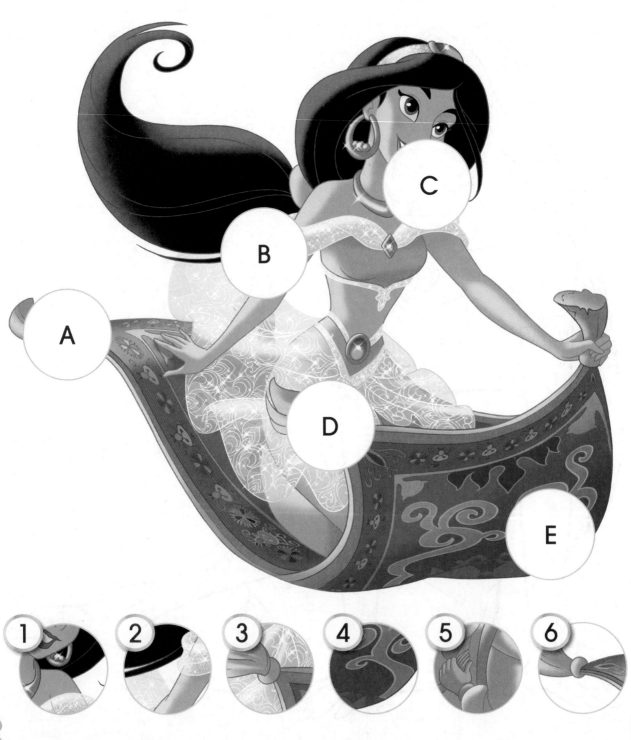

Answers on page 48

Jasmine Dress-up

Jasmine wants to go and explore the kingdom. Use stickers from your sticker sheet to dress her in a beautiful outfit.

A Winter Dance

Colour in this picture of Cinderella and her prince using your best pens and pencils.

Flower Design

Cinderella has been picking flowers.
Can you design a beautiful bouquet for her?

Royal Ball

Belle is planning a ball for all her friends and family.
Help her by filling in the details on the invitation.

Dear guest,

I would be honoured if you would attend my

Royal Ball

It will be held at:

....

(Think of an enchanting venue)

The date will be:

....

(What day of the week will it be?)

The dress code is:

....

(What should guests wear?)

Please RSVP to
Princess Belle

Sticker Dressing

What should Belle wear to the ball? Help her get ready.
Use your stickers to add some gloves and shoes.

Which Path?

Aurora is looking for the three fairies, Flora, Fauna and Merryweather. Which path should she take to find them?

Answer on page 48

Aurora Dress-up

Aurora has a busy day ahead of her. Use your stickers to complete her dress and give her a basket to carry.

Merida Dress-up

Merida needs to get ready for action. Use the stickers from your sheet to add her bow, arrows, shoes and friendly bird.

Highland Colouring

Merida is brave enough to follow her dreams.
Colour in this picture of the Princess.

Ariel's Treasures

Look at the list of items. Can you spot these four things in Princess Ariel's bedroom? Circle each one when you find it.

- Hair comb
- Purple cushion
- Umbrella
- Pair of slippers

Secrets of the Sea

Follow Ariel beneath the waves! Draw an enchanting underwater scene and then colour it in.

My Favourite Princess

Who is your favourite Disney Princess? Add the rest of the princesses to the page using your small square stickers. Now circle your favourite and write about her below.

I like this princess because...

_____

_____

_____

_____

_____

Answers

Page 3

Page 4
A – bird, B – butterfly,
C – frog, D – rabbit

Page 5

Page 6

Page 8

1. 2. 3. 4.

Page 9

Page 10
C and D are the matching pair

Page 11
A-3, B-2, C-4, D-1

Page 12
C is the correct path

Page 14
E, D, F, A, C, B

Page 17
There are eight butterflies

Page 21
1. True
2. False – she has three little
   brothers, who are triplets
3. False – his name is Angus
4. True
5. True

47

Answers

Page 23

Page 25
A-3, B-4, C-2, D-1

Page 27

Page 30
1. Seven
2. Four
3. Red

Page 31
HAPPY

Page 32
A-1, B-3, C-2, D-4

Page 34
A-6, B-2, C-1, D-3, E-4
5 does not belong

Page 40
B is the correct path

Page 44